Storms

Heera Kang • Illustrated by Drew Rose

Contents

Rigby

A Harcourt Achieve Imprint

www.Rigby.com
1-800-531-5015

Prairie Hills Elementary
Literacy Resource

Stormy Tales

"Wow, Vince," said Tuan, panting. "You guys really do get some crazy weather around here."

It was true. Vince couldn't believe their bad luck. The sun had been shining all morning as they looked for toads by the pond. They found the toads—but then they lost the sun!

Vince led the group as they dashed toward his house to escape the downpour. Tuan and John followed close behind.

Finally making it into the house, they rushed to the large window in the living room to watch the storm grow stronger.

Vince couldn't believe it. His friends had come to visit him for the weekend, and it was raining! Tuan and John had flown all the way from southern California, where it's warm and sunny almost every day. Vince and his family used to live there, too. The three friends had grown up together until Vince's family moved to Texas last month. It was his friends' first visit, and now they were stuck indoors!

"Is it just me, or does it sound like those little toads out there are croaking as hard as they can?" asked John.

They all pressed their faces against the window. They had a great view of the pond, and it really did seem like all of the toads were croaking at the same time. The boys stared in wonder.

"I heard a story once about toads and rain," said Tuan eagerly. "A long time ago, plants and animals were dying of thirst. There hadn't been rain in a long time. So one day this toad decided to do something about it. He went to ask the Thunder King for help."

John and Vince stared at Tuan with strange looks on their faces. They had no idea what their friend was talking about.

"Except the Thunder King was protected by all of these guards," continued Tuan. "Not everyone was allowed to walk in and talk to the king—especially not a toad!"

Tuan was thinking hard to remember the story. "The toad almost didn't go at all because he didn't think that one little toad could make a difference."

"But on the way to visit the Thunder King, a swarm of bees, a rooster, and a tiger joined the toad. You see, they were all dying of thirst, too," said Tuan.

At the mention of a tiger, John and Vince looked much more interested in the story.

"When they got to the king's palace, the bees swarmed and stung the guards. The rooster crowed as loud as he could, and the tiger tried his best to scare the guards away," said Tuan excitedly. "They helped that little toad get to the Thunder King to ask for rain."

"And?" asked John and Vince at the same time.

"Well, the king had heard how hard the toad had worked to see him," said Tuan. "He said that the toad didn't have to go through all that just to ask for rain. The toad should have just croaked as loud as he could, and the Thunder King would have heard him. That's why we hear toads croak before it rains!"

After Tuan finished the story, the three friends slowly turned back to the window. They watched the toads throw their little heads back and croak up to the skies.

"They're really loud," whispered John.

"I guess this means a lot more rain," sighed Vince.

BOOM! A loud crack of thunder startled the three friends, who jumped away from the window.

"Come and get some snacks, kids!" Vince's mother called as loud as thunder from the other room.

Vince sighed as he led his friends into the kitchen. His mom was always yelling from across the house.

"Mom, you're yelling like that mother sheep again," said Vince.

Vince's mom laughed. "I guess you're right."

Tuan and John looked at each other and shrugged. "Did we miss something?" asked Tuan.

"Well, there's a story about how at one time Thunder and Lightning were animals on Earth," said Vince. "Lightning was a young ram. He had a bad temper and liked to smash things and light them on fire."

"The ram went around the forest getting into trouble, and his mom was always yelling at him," said Vince. He gave his mom a playful look. "The ram's mom was Thunder."

"Why did the ram like to set things on fire?" asked John.

Tuan gave John a weary look. "It's a story, John. That's just what he did. Go on, Vince."

"OK, so the people didn't really like the ram lighting things on fire, right?" said Vince. "And they hated hearing his mom's booming voice yelling at him."

Vince described how the ram and his mother were finally sent to live up in the sky. The people thought that they had solved the problem, but they had only made it much worse.

"The ram became even meaner and learned how to send streams of fire from the sky down to Earth. And that's why we have lightning," Vince explained. "Every time the ram sends lightning, his mom yells at him to stop. And that's why we have thunder."

Just then a flash of lightning lit up the sky. It was followed by a crack of thunder that made all three friends look over at Mrs. Jordan.

"What are you looking at?" boomed Mrs. Jordan. Everybody laughed as she imitated a sheep and chased them around, yelling "Baaa!"

Vince, Tuan, and John spent most of the afternoon telling stories. Some stories they had heard before, and others they made up. Every time something new happened with the storm, someone would tell a story to explain why it had happened.

They sat quietly for a minute, trying to think of the next story.

"Butterflies," said John softly.

"Butterflies?" asked Tuan.

"Butterflies," said John again.

Tuan looked at Vince for an explanation, but Vince only shrugged.

"Yellow butterflies!" said John eagerly this time. "I heard that if you see yellow butterflies, it means that good weather—" John stopped speaking and stared out the window.

"That's not much of a story," said Tuan.

"It's not a story," John said. "I see some yellow butterflies outside!"

Tuan and Vince turned toward the window to see what John was looking at. Just as quickly as the storm had started, it was over. The sun shone brightly through the window, making the boys squint. A rainbow had formed in the distance.

The next minute, they were racing toward the door and pulling on their muddy shoes.

As the three friends ran outside, Vince decided that it wasn't so bad that Texas weather changed so suddenly. It was something that he couldn't control, but they had made the best of the afternoon anyway.

Vince started to think that things would be OK in this new place, just as long as he kept a close eye on the toads. Vince glanced over at the pond. The lily pads floated gently on the water, without a toad to be seen—or heard.

Chasing Storms

Storm chasers often have to drive hundreds of miles at a time just to get a good look at a tornado.

Storm chasers are people who study severe weather, such as **thunderstorms** and **tornadoes**. Some storm chasers are called **meteorologists**. They help local weather services get information that can help warn people when a storm is coming and how bad it will be.

At any given time, there are nearly 2,000 thunderstorms booming around the world. Someone, somewhere, is surely following many of these storms with cameras and other video recording equipment.

One challenge storm chasers face is trying to be at the right place at the right time. For example, some thunderstorms form tornadoes. Scientists aren't sure exactly why this happens, so storm chasers can't always use weather reports to guess where and when a tornado will strike. They have to study weather patterns and make an educated guess about which storms to follow.

Tools for Chasing a Storm

Storm chasers try to get as close to a storm as possible. How do they know where to go? How do they know how close they can get to a storm and still be safe? Preparing for a chase requires a lot of time, energy, and equipment.

One of the first things chasers need is a sturdy, four-wheel-drive vehicle. Storm chasers also need maps, weather reports, and instruments that measure wind, temperature, and distances. They need radio equipment to stay in touch with local weather services, cameras to take pictures and to videotape the storm, and journals to note the path of the storm. Road maps are important as well so storm chasers can get away quickly if the storm becomes too dangerous.

Why Chase When You Can Spot?

Storm spotters help look out for severe weather. Unlike storm chasers, storm spotters don't drive around the country in search of storms. They stay close to home and are often trained as part of a program that reports local weather.

Groups like Skywarn, a team of national storm spotters, send people to watch storms in different places. These spotters report what they notice about the storms, such as **lightning** and wind speed. Skywarn then gives this information to the local National Weather Services forecast office. The information gives people in an area time to prepare for the storm.

⚡ Spotlight on Lightning

Did you know that a bolt of lightning is about five times hotter than the surface of the sun? Here's a way to figure out how far away lightning is from you.

1. During a storm, wait for a flash of lightning.
2. After the flash, count the number of seconds until the thunder booms.
3. Divide this number by five. The answer tells you how many miles away the lightning is.

Tornado Fever

A tornado is one of the most powerful weather events on Earth. These spinning pillars of air usually form during a thunderstorm, but neither scientists nor storm chasers know exactly when a tornado will strike.

Although tornadoes can be found all over the United States, there is an area called "Tornado Alley" that gets more tornadoes than any other part of the country. Tornado Alley stretches from North Dakota down to Louisiana and Texas. Storm chasers from all around come to Tornado Alley during "tornado season," which lasts from April to June.

This chart shows when most tornadoes strike the United States during a given year.

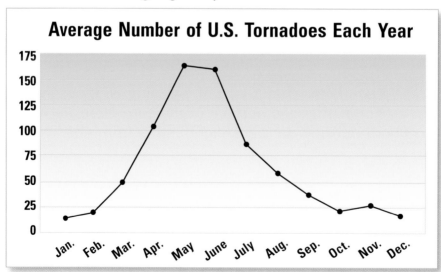

Average Number of U.S. Tornadoes Each Year

One of the most important moments in the history of tornado chasing happened during a tornado that hit Union City, Oklahoma, in 1973. Storm chasers worked with scientists who were using a new instrument with Doppler radar. The machine measures wind speed and direction. For the first time ever, scientists were able to record information about a tornado from beginning to end.

The Marshall County Tornado of 2005

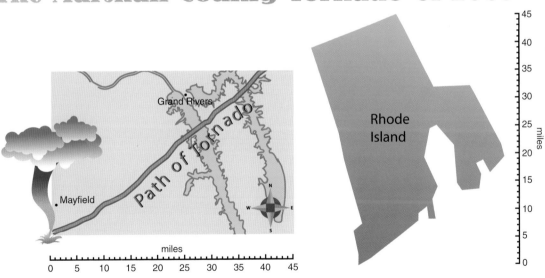

Grand Rivers

Path of Tornado

Mayfield

miles
0 5 10 15 20 25 30 35 40 45

Rhode Island

miles
45
40
35
30
25
20
15
10
5
0

The longest recorded distance that a tornado traveled on the ground is 44.1 miles. This was the Marshall County, Kentucky, Tornado of 2005. If this tornado had hit Rhode Island, it would have traveled through the whole state.

Hurricane Hunters

Storm chasers are good at spotting lightning and tornadoes, but they aren't able to track storms over the ocean, like **hurricanes**. Hurricanes are huge storms that can be several hundred miles across and have wind speeds of 75 to 200 miles per hour

Since storm chasers can't track hurricanes from the ground, a group of pilots called the "Hurricane Hunters" takes over. These pilots help gather information by flying directly into the eye of the hurricane, which is the very center of the storm that is mostly calm with light winds. The National Hurricane Center studies this information and figures out the size and strength of the hurricane and where it will travel.

This satellite image shows a hurricane off the coast of Florida.

On the Front Line of a Storm

Even with new computers and equipment, people will never be able to control the weather. The most we can try to do is study bad weather and track it early on.

People who follow the weather understand the power of a storm. Tornadoes can reach speeds of almost 300 miles per hour. A hurricane can destroy entire communities at a time. One bolt of lightning can burn down a house.

Hurricane Hunters and storm chasers have dangerous jobs, but the information they gather for weather scientists has saved many homes and lives. As long as there are storms, there will be storm chasers on the lookout!

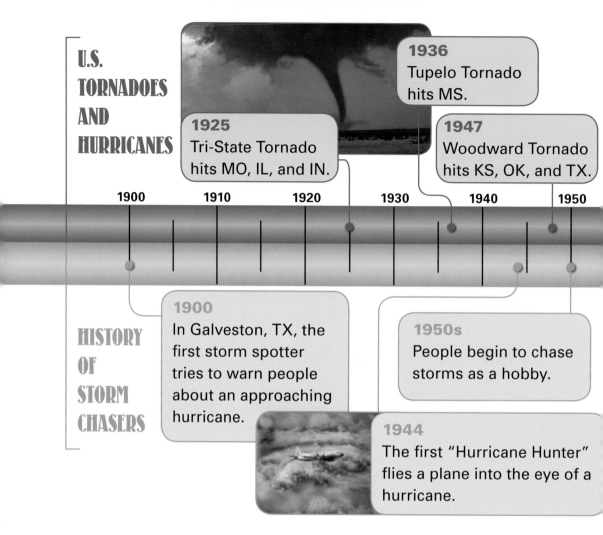

U.S. TORNADOES AND HURRICANES

1925
Tri-State Tornado hits MO, IL, and IN.

1936
Tupelo Tornado hits MS.

1947
Woodward Tornado hits KS, OK, and TX.

1900 1910 1920 1930 1940 1950

HISTORY OF STORM CHASERS

1900
In Galveston, TX, the first storm spotter tries to warn people about an approaching hurricane.

1944
The first "Hurricane Hunter" flies a plane into the eye of a hurricane.

1950s
People begin to chase storms as a hobby.

The Shape of the Cloud Tells All

Learning the different shapes of clouds and what kind of weather each will bring is an important skill for weather watchers. Storm chasers look out for cumulonimbus clouds, which are also called thunderstorm clouds. These clouds grow up and down and usually mean that a storm is on the way.

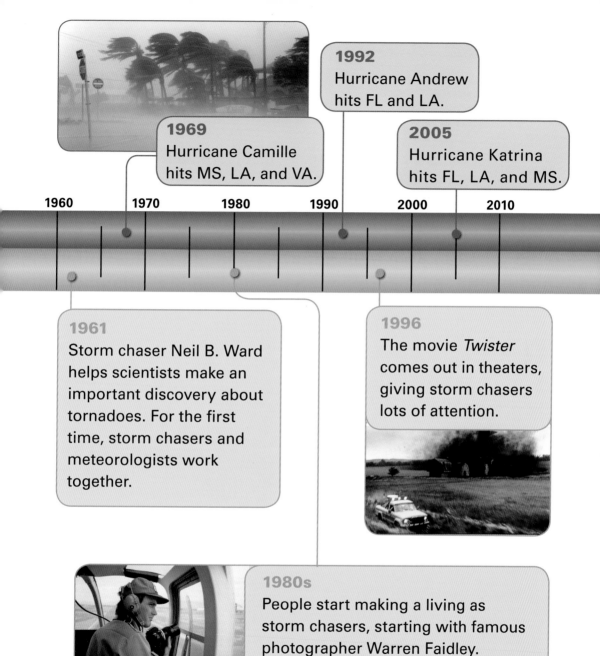

1969
Hurricane Camille hits MS, LA, and VA.

1992
Hurricane Andrew hits FL and LA.

2005
Hurricane Katrina hits FL, LA, and MS.

1960   1970   1980   1990   2000   2010

1961
Storm chaser Neil B. Ward helps scientists make an important discovery about tornadoes. For the first time, storm chasers and meteorologists work together.

1996
The movie *Twister* comes out in theaters, giving storm chasers lots of attention.

1980s
People start making a living as storm chasers, starting with famous photographer Warren Faidley.

 Glossary

hurricane a severe tropical storm with heavy
rains and winds
lightning a bolt of electricity that is formed
during a thunderstorm
meteorologist a person who reports and
studies the weather
storm chaser a person who chases thunderstorms
and severe weather
storm spotter a person who stays near a
community and reports weather that could
become severe storms
thunderstorm rainy weather with lightning
and thunder
tornado spinning pillars of air during
a thunderstorm

Index